FLOWER
COLORING BOOK
FOR ADULTS VOL 2

Preview of Coloring Pages

www.arttherapycoloring.com

Preview of Coloring Pages

cactus & succulents

Test Your Colors

Drawings

Drawings

Best Selling Art Therapy Coloring Books

Coloring Books For Adults:

- Zombie Coloring Book: Black Background
- Butterfly Coloring Book For Adults: Black Background
- Tattoo Coloring Book: Black Background
- Coloring Books for Adults Relaxation: Native American Inspired Designs
- Fishing Coloring Book for Adults: Black Background

Coloring Books For Men:

- Coloring Book for Men: Anti-Stress Designs Vol 1
- Coloring Book For Men: Fishing Designs
- Coloring Book For Men: Tattoo Designs
- Coloring Books for Men: Hunting
- Coloring Book For Men: Biker Designs

Coloring Books For Seniors:

- Coloring Book For Seniors: Nature Designs Vol 1
- Coloring Book For Seniors: Anti-Stress Designs Vol 1
- Coloring Books for Seniors: Relaxing Designs
- Coloring Book For Seniors: Floral Designs Vol 1
- Coloring Book For Seniors: Ocean Designs Vol 1

Coloring Books For Teens and Tweens:

- Coloring Books For Teens: Ocean Designs
- Coloring Books for Teen Girls Vol 1
- Teen Inspirational Coloring Books
- Coloring Book for Teens: Anti-Stress Designs Vol 1
- Tween Coloring Books For Girls: Cute Animals

Coloring Books For Kids:

- Horse Coloring Book For Girls
- Coloring Books For Boys: Sharks
- Coloring Books for Boys: Animal Designs
- Unicorn Coloring Book for Girls
- Detailed Coloring Books For Kids

Art Therapy Coloring Books

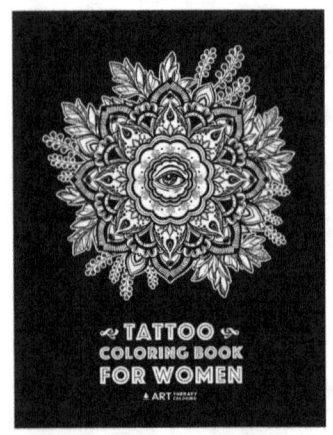

TATTOO
COLORING BOOK
FOR WOMEN

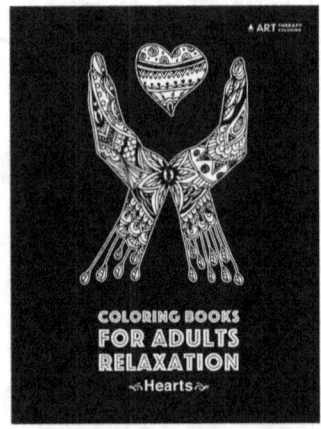

COLORING BOOKS
FOR ADULTS
RELAXATION
Hearts

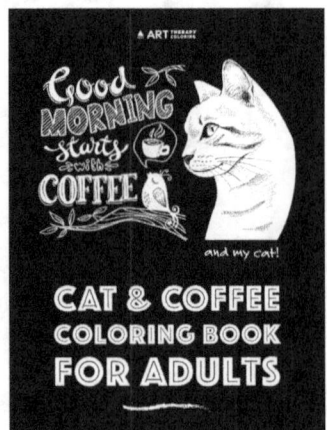

Good MORNING starts with COFFEE
and my cat!
CAT & COFFEE
COLORING BOOK
FOR ADULTS

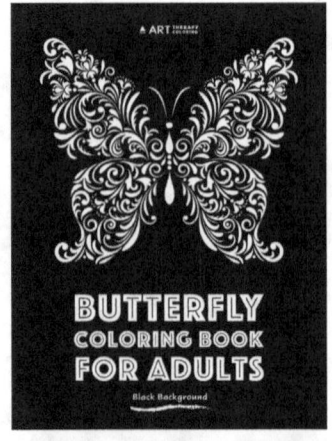

BUTTERFLY
COLORING BOOK
FOR ADULTS
Black Background

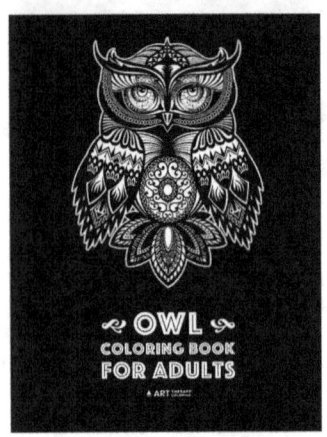

OWL
COLORING BOOK
FOR ADULTS

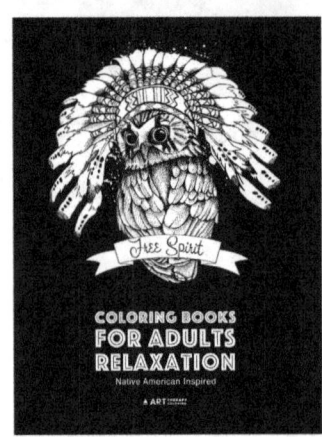

Free Spirit
COLORING BOOKS
FOR ADULTS
RELAXATION
Native American Inspired

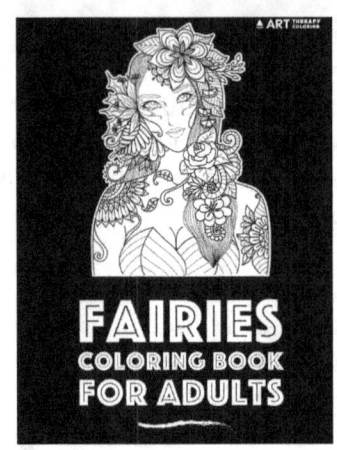

FAIRIES
COLORING BOOK
FOR ADULTS

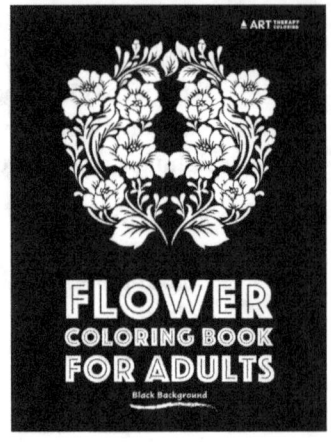

FLOWER
COLORING BOOK
FOR ADULTS
Black Background

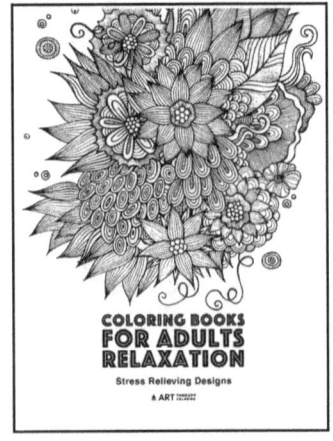

COLORING BOOKS
FOR ADULTS
RELAXATION
Stress Relieving Designs

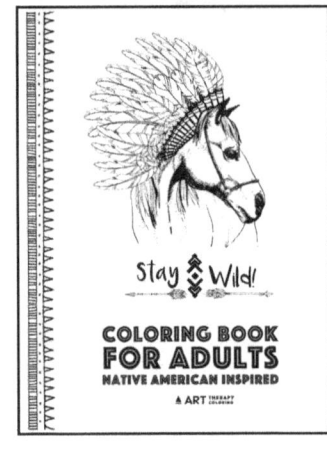

Stay Wild!
COLORING BOOK
FOR ADULTS
NATIVE AMERICAN INSPIRED

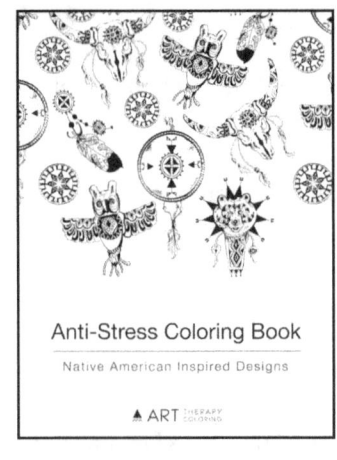

Anti-Stress Coloring Book
Native American Inspired Designs

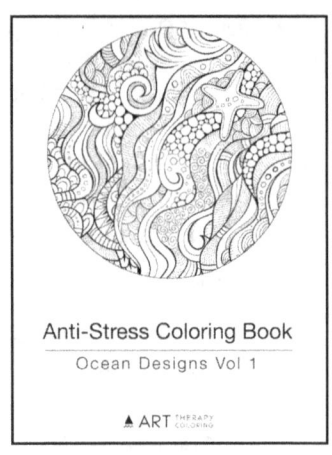

Anti-Stress Coloring Book
Ocean Designs Vol 1

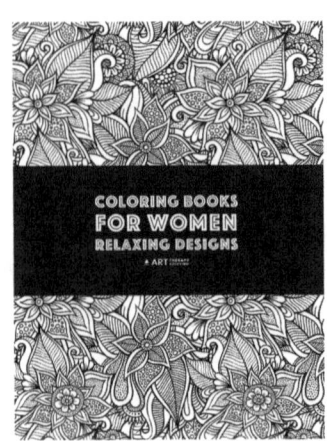

COLORING BOOKS
FOR WOMEN
RELAXING DESIGNS

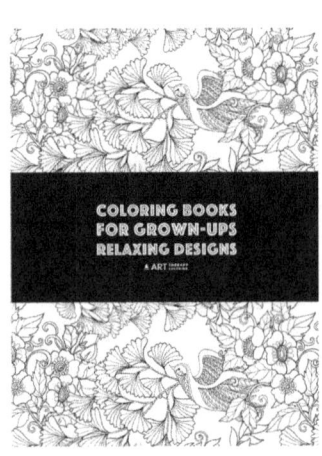

COLORING BOOKS
FOR GROWN-UPS
RELAXING DESIGNS

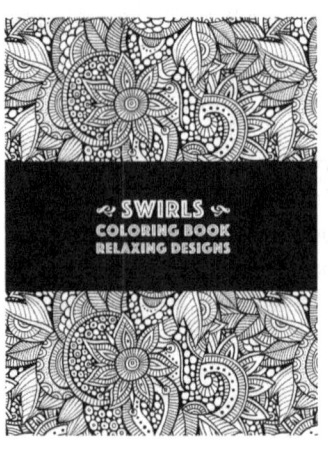

SWIRLS
COLORING BOOK
RELAXING DESIGNS

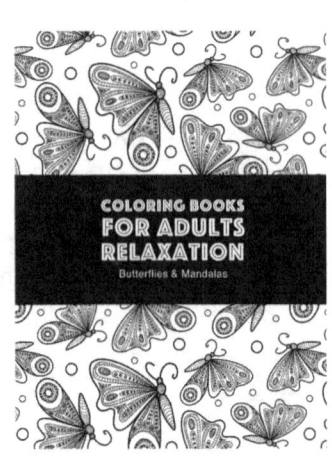

COLORING BOOKS
FOR ADULTS
RELAXATION
Butterflies & Mandalas

Art Therapy Coloring Books

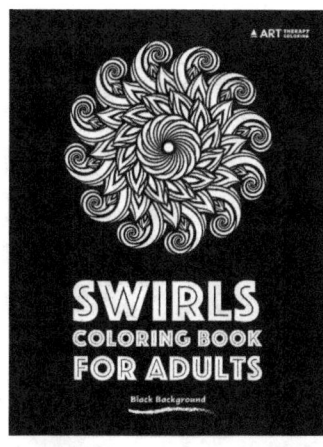

SWIRLS
COLORING BOOK FOR ADULTS
Black Background

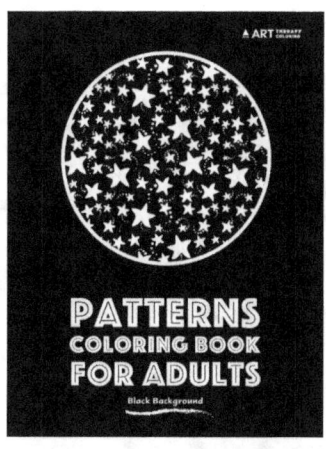

PATTERNS
COLORING BOOK FOR ADULTS
Black Background

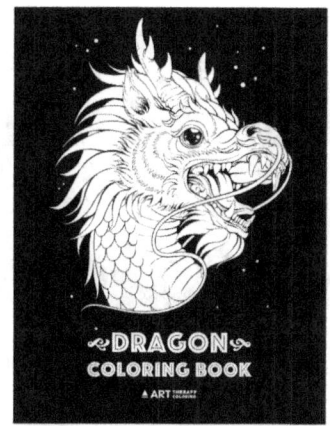

DRAGON
COLORING BOOK

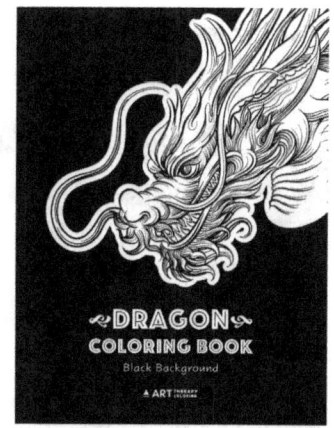

DRAGON
COLORING BOOK
Black Background

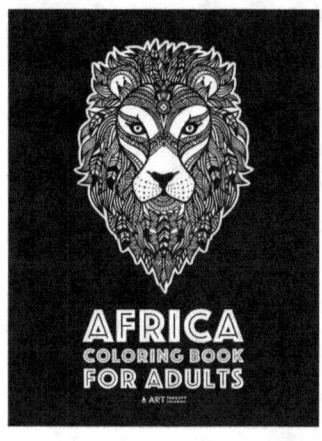

AFRICA
COLORING BOOK FOR ADULTS

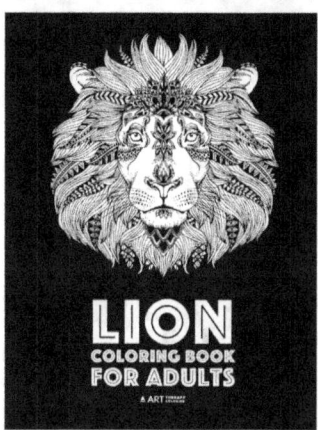

LION
COLORING BOOK FOR ADULTS

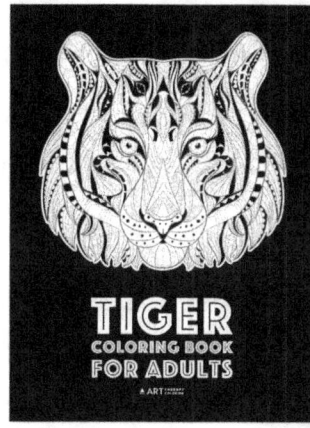

TIGER
COLORING BOOK FOR ADULTS

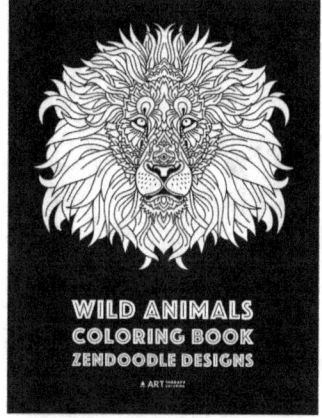

WILD ANIMALS
COLORING BOOK ZENDOODLE DESIGNS

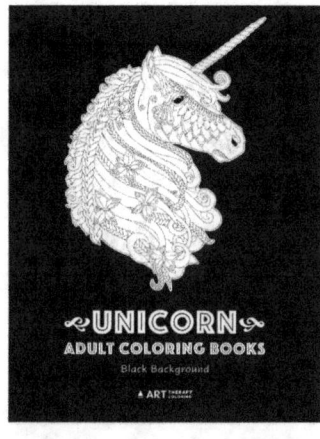

UNICORN
ADULT COLORING BOOKS
Black Background

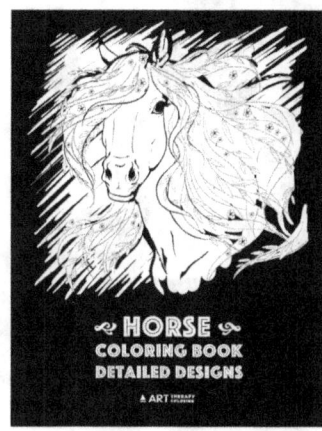

HORSE
COLORING BOOK DETAILED DESIGNS

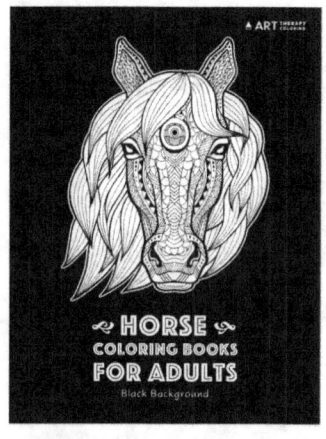

HORSE
COLORING BOOKS FOR ADULTS
Black Background

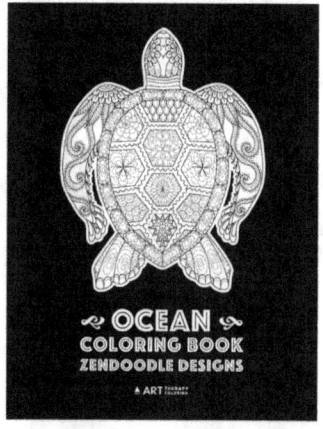

OCEAN
COLORING BOOK ZENDOODLE DESIGNS

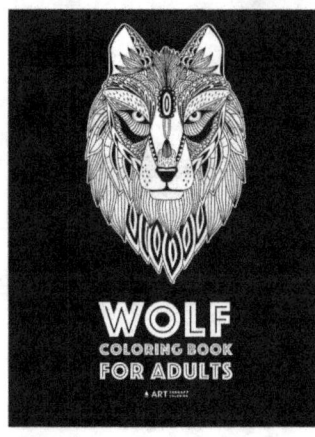

WOLF
COLORING BOOK FOR ADULTS

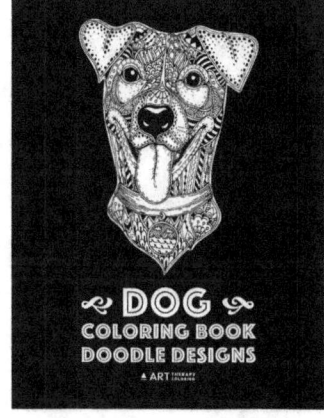

DOG
COLORING BOOK DOODLE DESIGNS

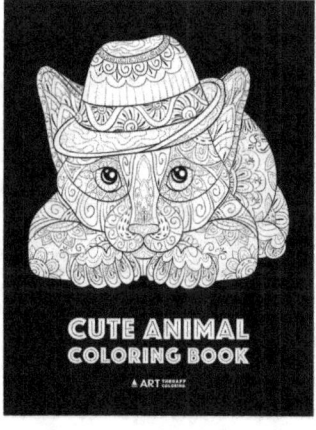

CUTE ANIMAL
COLORING BOOK

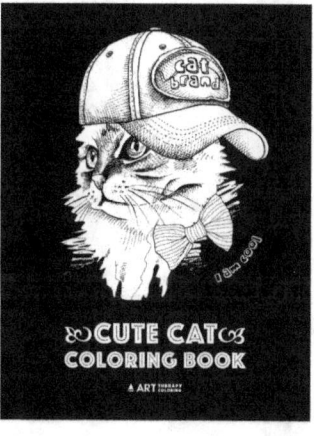

CUTE CAT
COLORING BOOK

Art Therapy Coloring Books

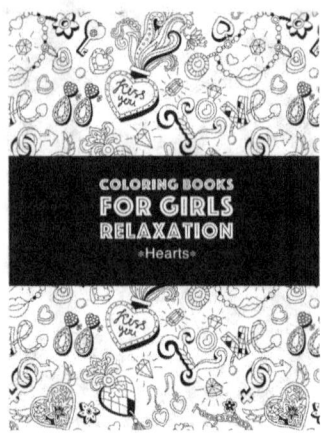

Art Therapy Coloring Books

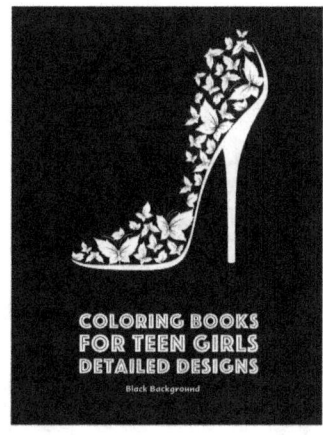

COLORING BOOKS
FOR TEEN GIRLS
DETAILED DESIGNS

Black Background

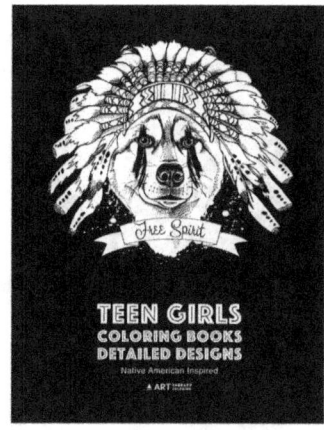

TEEN GIRLS
COLORING BOOKS
DETAILED DESIGNS

Native American Inspired

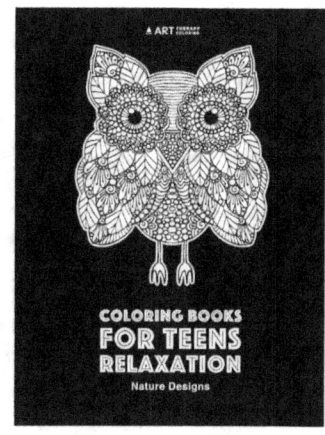

COLORING BOOKS
FOR TEENS
RELAXATION

Nature Designs

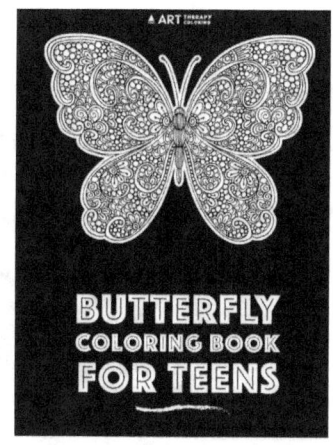

BUTTERFLY
COLORING BOOK
FOR TEENS

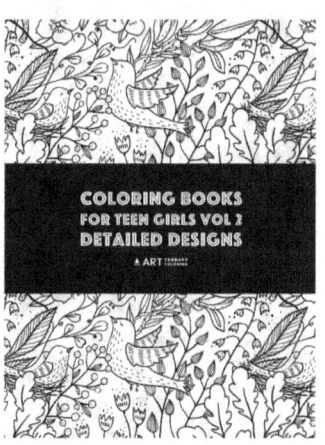

COLORING BOOKS
FOR TEEN GIRLS VOL 2
DETAILED DESIGNS

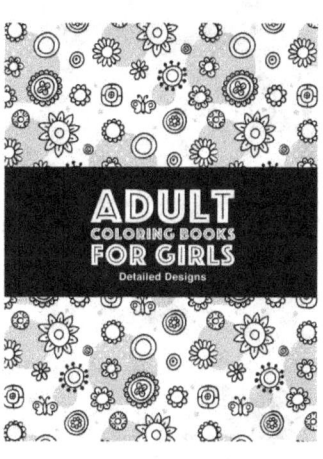

ADULT
COLORING BOOKS
FOR GIRLS

Detailed Designs

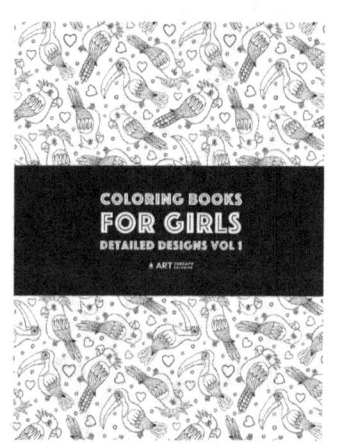

COLORING BOOKS
FOR GIRLS
DETAILED DESIGNS VOL 1

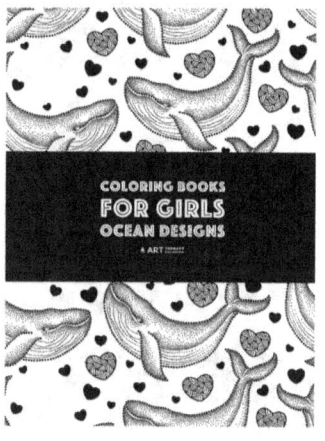

COLORING BOOKS
FOR GIRLS
OCEAN DESIGNS

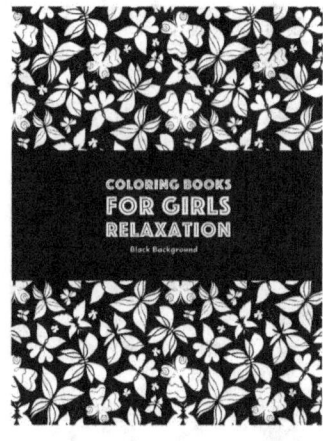

COLORING BOOKS
FOR GIRLS
RELAXATION

Black Background

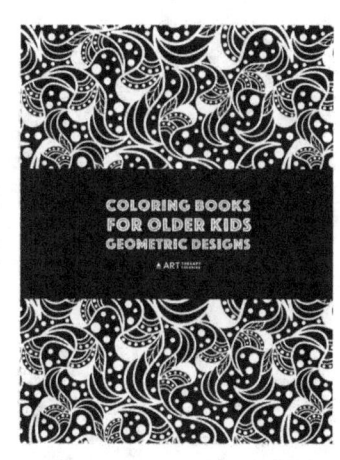

COLORING BOOKS
FOR OLDER KIDS
GEOMETRIC DESIGNS

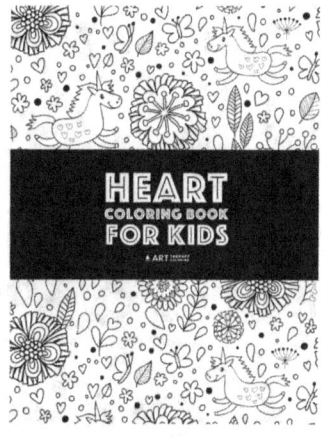

HEART
COLORING BOOK
FOR KIDS

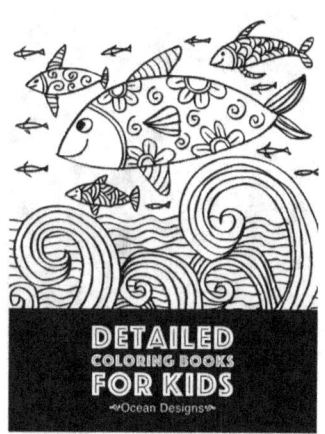

DETAILED
COLORING BOOKS
FOR KIDS

Ocean Designs

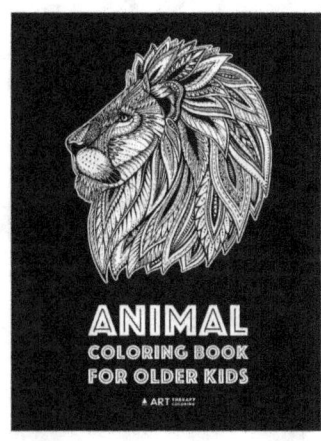

ANIMAL
COLORING BOOK
FOR OLDER KIDS

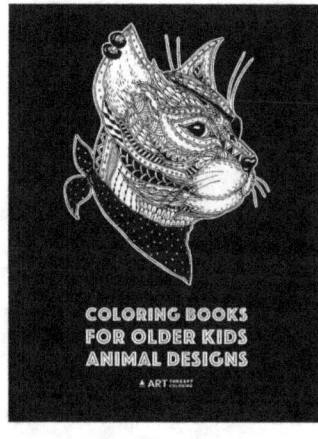

COLORING BOOKS
FOR OLDER KIDS
ANIMAL DESIGNS

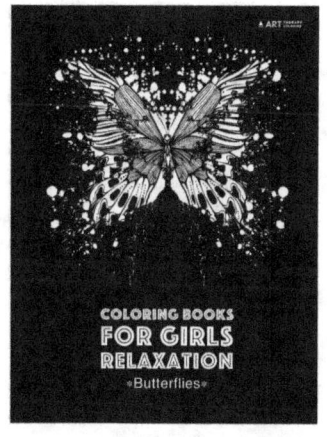

COLORING BOOKS
FOR GIRLS
RELAXATION

Butterflies

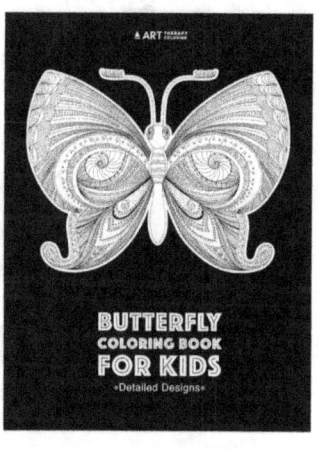

BUTTERFLY
COLORING BOOK
FOR KIDS

Detailed Designs

Art Therapy Coloring Books

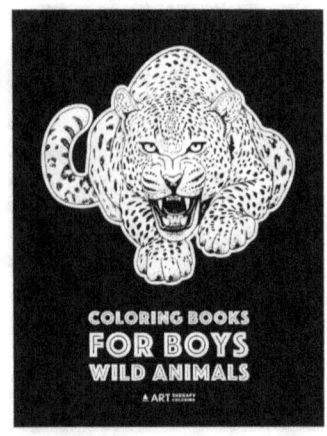

COLORING BOOKS FOR BOYS WILD ANIMALS

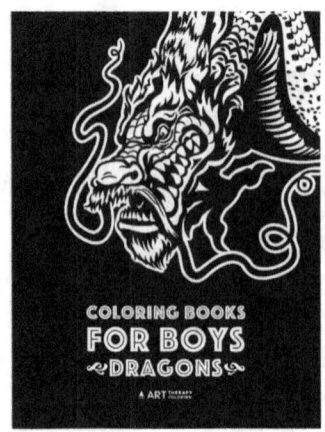

COLORING BOOKS FOR BOYS DRAGONS

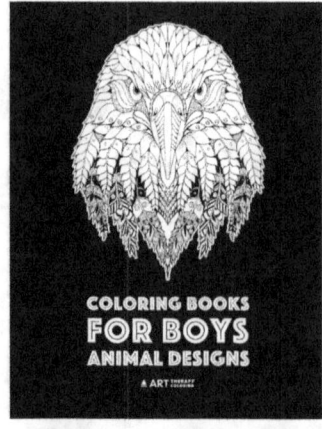

COLORING BOOKS FOR BOYS ANIMAL DESIGNS

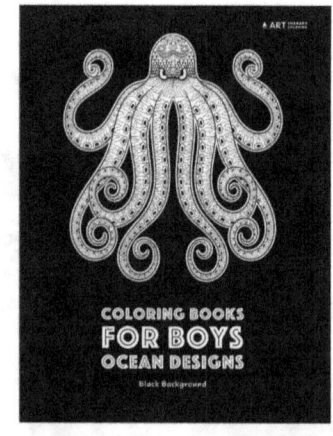

COLORING BOOKS FOR BOYS OCEAN DESIGNS
Black Background

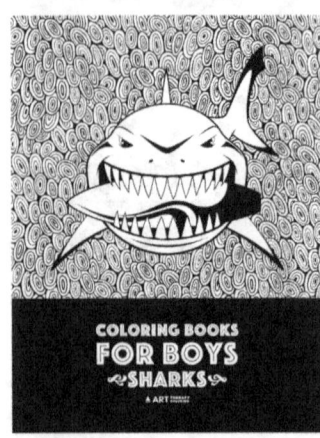

COLORING BOOKS FOR BOYS SHARKS

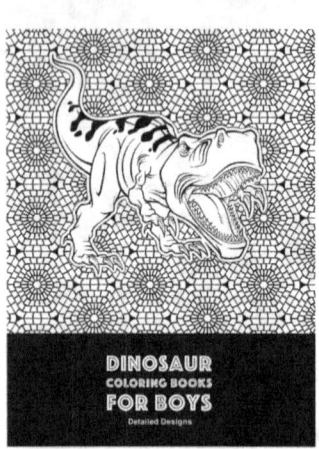

DINOSAUR COLORING BOOKS FOR BOYS
Detailed Designs

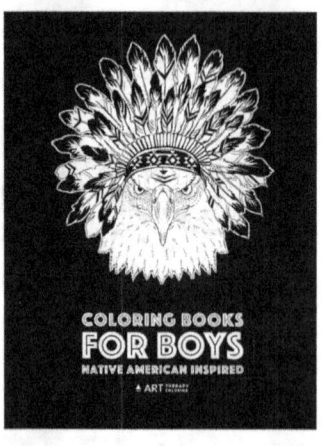

COLORING BOOKS FOR BOYS NATIVE AMERICAN INSPIRED

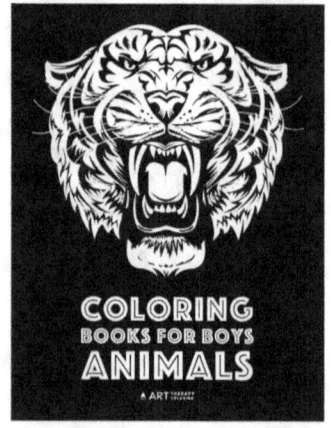

COLORING BOOKS FOR BOYS ANIMALS

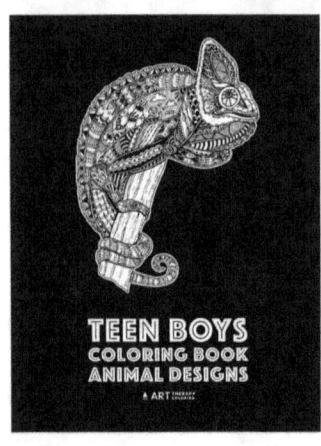

TEEN BOYS COLORING BOOK ANIMAL DESIGNS

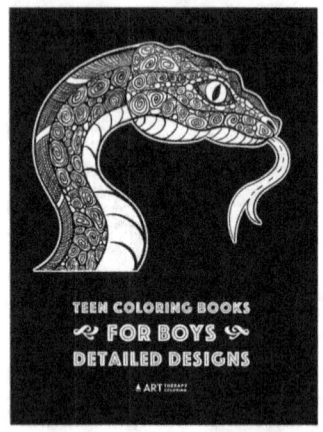

TEEN COLORING BOOKS FOR BOYS DETAILED DESIGNS

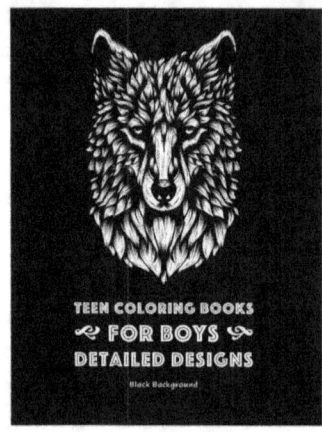

TEEN COLORING BOOKS FOR BOYS DETAILED DESIGNS
Black Background

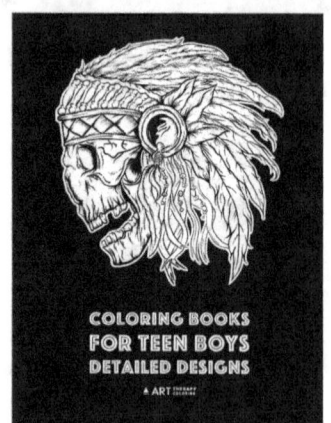

COLORING BOOKS FOR TEEN BOYS DETAILED DESIGNS

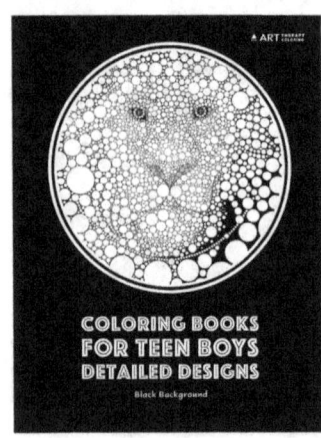

COLORING BOOKS FOR TEEN BOYS DETAILED DESIGNS
Black Background

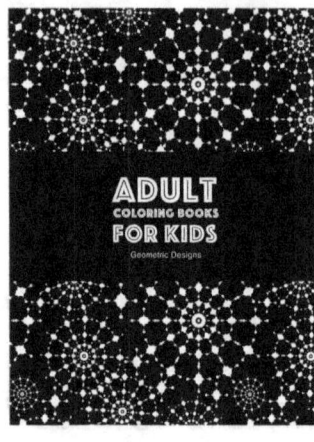

ADULT COLORING BOOKS FOR KIDS
Geometric Designs

ROBOT COLORING BOOK DETAILED DESIGNS

DETAILED COLORING BOOKS FOR KIDS
Geometric Designs

Art Therapy Coloring Books

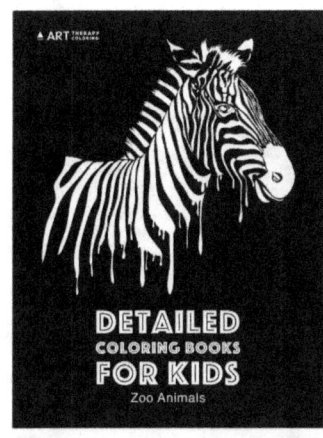

DETAILED COLORING BOOKS **FOR KIDS** Zoo Animals

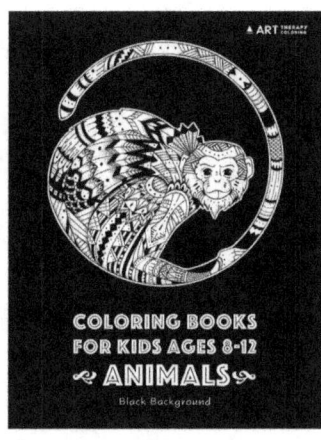

COLORING BOOKS FOR KIDS AGES 8-12 **ANIMALS** Black Background

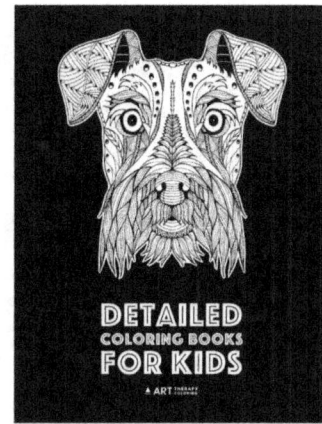

DETAILED COLORING BOOKS **FOR KIDS**

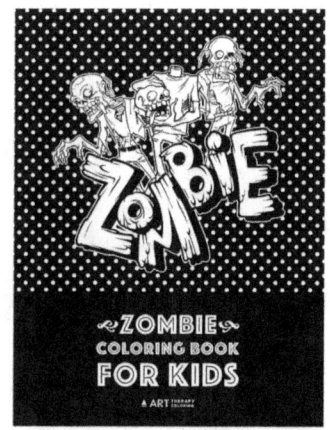

ZOMBIE COLORING BOOK **FOR KIDS**

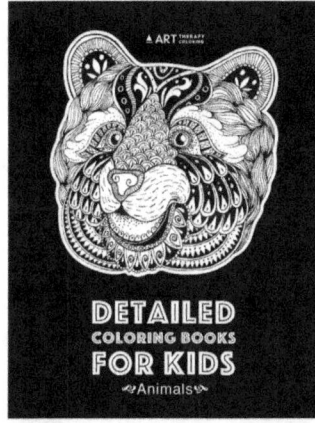

DETAILED COLORING BOOKS **FOR KIDS** Animals

DETAILED COLORING BOOKS **FOR KIDS** Elephants

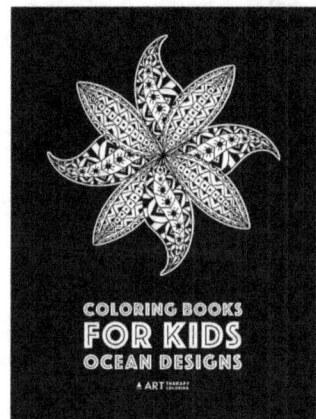

COLORING BOOKS **FOR KIDS** OCEAN DESIGNS

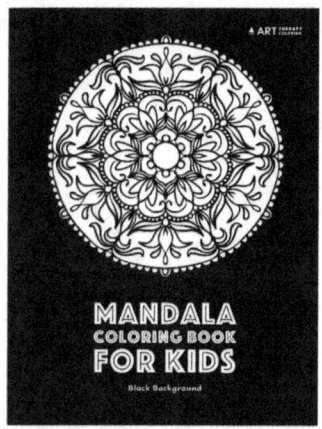

MANDALA COLORING BOOK **FOR KIDS** Black Background

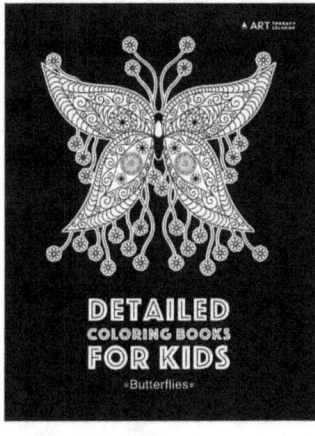

DETAILED COLORING BOOKS **FOR KIDS** Butterflies

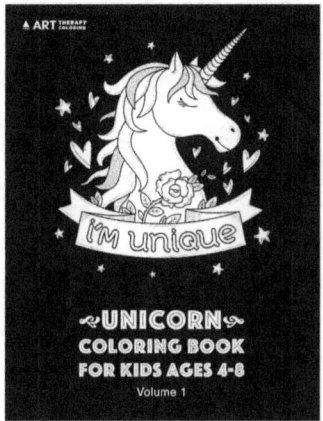

UNICORN COLORING BOOK FOR KIDS AGES 4-8 Volume 1

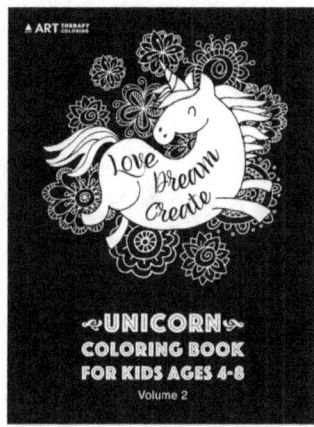

UNICORN COLORING BOOK FOR KIDS AGES 4-8 Volume 2

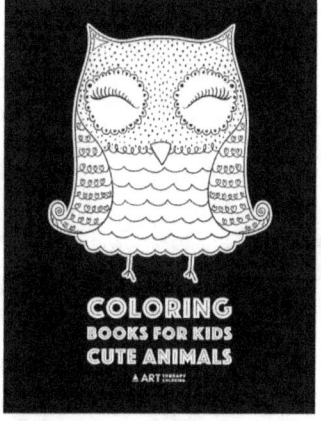

COLORING BOOKS FOR KIDS CUTE ANIMALS

KIDS MANDALA COLORING BOOK

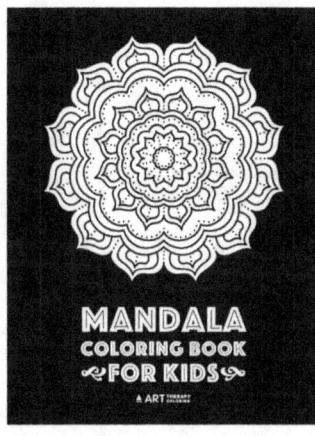

MANDALA COLORING BOOK **FOR KIDS**

SHARK COLORING BOOK

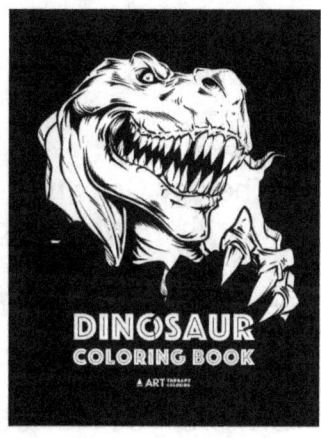

DINOSAUR COLORING BOOK

Flower Coloring Book
For Adults Vol 2

Published by:
Art Therapy Coloring
www.arttherapycoloring.com

ISBN: 978-1-944427-56-6